Animal Lives

THE LIFE OF A CAT

by Jan Feder

Illustrated by Tilman Michalski

CHILDRENS PRESS INTERNATIONAL
CHICAGO

Library of Congress Cataloging in Publication Data

Feder, Jan.
   The life of a cat.

   (Animal lives)
   Translation of: Die Katze.
   Summary: Text and photographs describe the day-
to-day life of a farm cat as she hunts for food,
mates, gives birth, and cares for her kittens.
Also includes general information about the
physical characteristics, habits, behavior, and
relationship to humans of the domestic cat.
   1. Cats—Juvenile literature. [1. Cats]
I. Michalski, Tilman, ill. II. Title. III. Series.
SF445.7.F413 1982   636.8   82-12795
ISBN 0-516-08931-58   AACR2

North American 1982 Edition published
by Regensteiner Publishing Enterprises, Inc.

Tabby the cat lived on a farm. Sometimes she slept in the farmhouse and was fed by the people. But usually she looked after herself.

Tabby was a good hunter. Most days she caught mice in the barn. But today she was going hunting in the fields.

Tabby hadn't gone far when suddenly she heard a sound. She froze. Then, silently, she moved closer and closer. It was a whitethroat.

She gave a sudden swift leap—but the bird was faster. Tabby's breakfast had escaped. She sat down crossly and washed her face.

Tabby was careful with birds anyway. She had caught a sparrow once. She plucked out most of its feathers before eating it. But she missed one of the little ones and it stuck in her throat. She had to cough and cough to get rid of it.

Tabby wandered back to the barn. There were plenty of mice there. They came to steal the grain. Sometimes Tabby caught five or six in a single night, and left them outside the farmhouse door.

Tabby had very good hearing. She could hear one squeaking now. She waited patiently, then suddenly pounced. She killed the mouse by biting through the back of its neck. It was all over very quickly.

The farmyard and the fields around it were Tabby's own territory. She had marked it with her scent. Neighboring cats could walk through it, but not hunt there.

The cats avoided each other by day. But in the late evening they often gathered and sat together, in silence.

One night Tabby began yowling and running around. She wanted a male cat to come to the farm. She knew it was time for her to mate and have kittens.

The tom cat from the next farm arrived, and he and Tabby mated. Afterward Tabby sent him away again.

About two months later Tabby's kittens were due. As she grew bigger she had found it harder to chase up trees or catch mice. She ate flies and beetles most of the time.

She could have eaten at the farmhouse. But she stayed away, and slept in the barn.

When the kittens were about to be born, Tabby made herself a nest in the straw. It was warm and dry. It was safe from the dog and the people of the farm. She would give birth to the kittens there.

One morning Tabby had her kittens, five of them. They were blind and helpless. They immediately began to drink their mother's milk. They gently pressed with their paws to make the milk flow.

Tabby was a good mother. She left her kittens only when she needed to eat.

A week or so later the kittens began to open their eyes. When Tabby was there to watch they explored outside the nest.

Tabby left them more often now. She had started to hunt mice again. She brought back insects and beetles for the kittens, who wanted solid food as well as milk.

Then Tabby started to bring back live mice. At first the kittens played with them. They did not know what else to do. But Tabby taught them how to kill, with a swift bite.

Gradually the kittens grew bigger and bolder.

When they were about three months old Tabby took the kittens hunting for the first time. They had so much to learn! They managed to catch some bumblebees and butterflies.

The kittens kept away from people. If they heard anyone coming they rushed back to the safety of the barn.

One day one of the kittens met the farmyard dog. It was so frightened it ran. That was a mistake, for the dog chased it. The poor kitten managed to leap onto a high fence and it stayed there until the dog gave up and went away.

The kittens had been growing fast. By now they were young cats. They were almost as strong as their mother and well able to look after themselves. Tabby began to drive them away from her territory. This puzzled them at first. But it was time for them to find homes, or territories, of their own.

Tabby started to go to the farmhouse again. It was getting colder. The barn was not as warm as the farmhouse on a chilly autumn evening.

And when winter came she would stay indoors most of the time, enjoying the warmth and comfort.

The Domestic Cat

How the cat came to live with human beings

Our human ancestors were hunters first. Then they became farmers. They built huts and houses where they could live and store food, especially the grain they grew. Mice soon came along to eat the grain, and cats followed the mice.

We cannot say exactly when cats came to live with people as household animals. Archaeological finds show that it must have been about eight thousand years ago, around 6,000 B.C. About 1,000 B.C. cats were worshiped in Egypt. The Egyptians considered cats sacred animals.

At this time, farmers in Europe were still keeping tame weasels, not cats, to catch mice. So we think that the ancestor of the domestic cat was not the European Wild Cat (now found only in Scotland and some other parts of Europe), but the Caffre Cat of Africa. Cats have been kept as useful domestic animals for centuries now. They keep houses, stables, and barns free of vermin. Insects, beetles, mice, and even rats are vermin. It is only over the last hundred years that people have been breeding pedigree cats for cat shows.

A relation of the lion

Lions, leopards, tigers, and pumas are related to the domestic cat. They are known as the big cats. The domestic cat is one of the small cats, but they all belong to the Felidae, the scientific name for the cat family. The Felidae are all beasts of prey (hunters). The domestic cat is naturally a nocturnal animal that hunts by night and sleeps by day. It can climb, stalk its prey and leap very nimbly. Its natural food consists of insects, birds, and small rodents, especially mice. Occasionally it eats grass, but this is thought to clear away balls of hair that the cat has swallowed while washing itself.

A small beast of prey

The cat is a hunter. The shape of its jaw helps it to deal with its prey. It has six small incisors, or cutting teeth, and two large curved canine teeth, at the front in both upper and lower jaws. Cats grip their prey with the incisors and canines, and tear it apart by shaking it. They cut and chew the meat with their molars, which are along the sides of the mouth. They act like scissor blades. Cats have rough tongues to clean shreds of meat from the bones.

The cat's most important weapons are its paws, which have sharp, curved claws. When cats are running or stalking their prey, their claws are drawn in or "retracted." Then they run almost silently on their well-padded paws. Only when they attack do their claws flash out at lightning speed.

When a cat jumps, or falls from a height, it steers itself with its tail. The tail is important because it helps the cat keep its balance.

The cat's senses

Being beasts of prey, cats have a naturally good sense of smell, although in fact they do not make very much use of it when they are hunting. It is used more when they are eating, or in company with other cats, or with humans.

Cats also have extremely good eyesight. They see six times as keenly as we do. Their eyes adjust much faster to light and darkness. The size of the pupil in the cat's eye changes, in much the same way as the aperture of a camera is adjusted. In bright light, the pupil narrows to a slit. When it gets darker, the pupil opens wider to take in more light. However, even cats cannot see in complete darkness.

The cat has a reflecting layer behind the retina of its eye that throws back light. This is why cats' eyes sometimes seem to be shining in the dark.

Cats see in color (some animals can only see in black and white). They have very keen hearing, too. They can turn their ears in any direction to pick up a sound. Cats' whiskers are another sense organ. They react to being touched. The spread of a cat's whiskers measures about the same as the width of its body. It is sometimes

The Cat and its Body

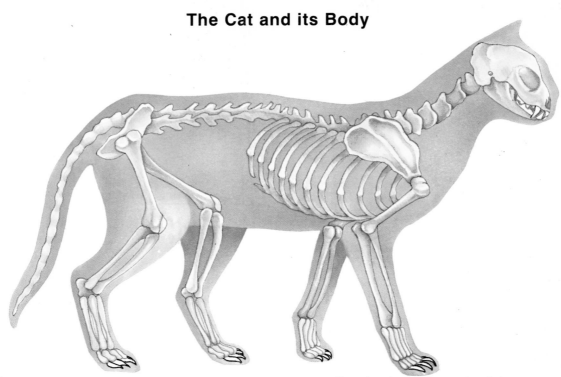

We can see that cats are very agile creatures from the structure of their bodies. The cat's backbone allows it to bend easily. Its forelegs and hind legs are set well under the body, and point inwards, so cats can run and keep their balance on narrow ledges. They use their tails for steering and balancing themselves.

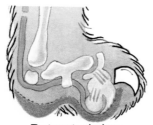

Retracted claw

Extended claw

Forepaw

Forepaw spread, with claws extended

Hind paw

thought that the whiskers tell a cat whether or not it can get through a narrow opening, although we are not quite sure about this theory.

Cats sometimes stalk, and kill, animals they do not eat. This is not just cruelty. A cat needs to have a strong desire to hunt because it may have to wait some time for a prey to stalk. A cat may stalk several prey before it manages to kill one. It would get very hungry, therefore if it did not start to hunt until it needed a meal.

A cat's territory

Apart from mating time, and the curious nighttime meetings when cats of the same neighborhood sit together in a silent gathering, the cat likes to live alone. It is a solitary animal. Each cat has its own hunting ground. It has favorite spots within this territory for resting and sleeping. The cat marks out its territory by leaving the scent of its urine and excreta on tree stumps, stones, and hummocks of earth. Sometimes the territories of several cats overlap. They will try to avoid meeting each other. Each cat will go hunting at a different time of day.

How cats reproduce

When mating time comes, the queens (females) who are in season (ready to mate) call out to the toms (males). Some of them may attract several toms with their cries, and then the toms fight. But the queen does not always choose the winner as her mate. Soon after mating, the queen drives the tom away again.

Her pregnancy lasts for sixty-five days. She has from two to six kittens. The newborn kittens are blind and helpless. They do not open their eyes for a week to ten days. At birth, kittens weigh 3.5 to 4.2 ounces (100 to 120 grams). The average weight of a grown cat is about 11 pounds (5 kilos). The kittens are suckled by their mother for seven or eight weeks. After that she brings freshly caught prey for them to eat. The kittens learn to know their natural prey from the food she brings

The Cat and its Prey

The cat pricks up its ears to listen – stalks its prey – catches sight of its prey – then attacks.

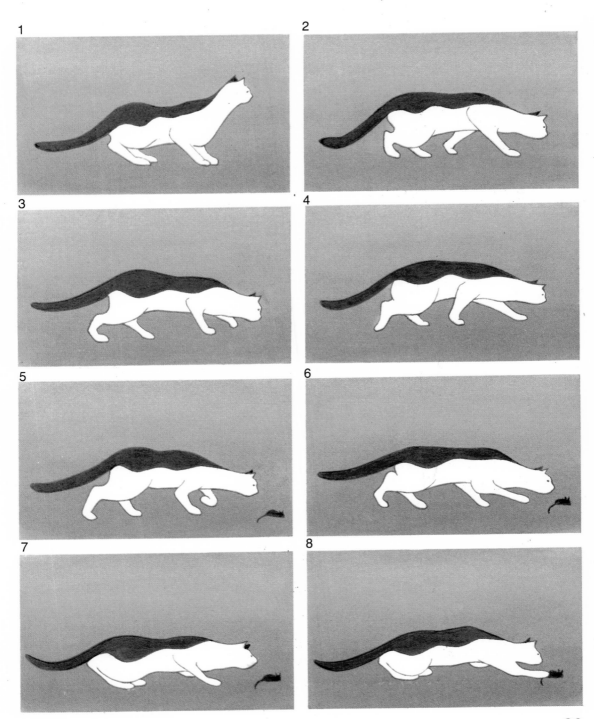

Varieties of Cat

Well-known varieties of short-haired and
long-haired cats

Red Abyssinian

Seal-point Siamese

Chartreux

European Shorthair

Russian Blue

Lilac-point
Siamese

Black Persian

White Persian

Tortoiseshell Persian

Red Persian

Smoke Persian

Rex

them, and from their own hunting expeditions with her a little later on. When they are as big as their mother, she drives them away. Cats can live to be 15 or 20 years old.

The cat and its language

It is not true that dogs and cats are natural enemies. However, they do use naturally different languages. That means they often misunderstand each other. When a dog lifts its paw and wags its tail it is saying, "Come and play with me." When a cat lifts its paw and waves its tail, it means, "Don't touch!" and a dog is bound to misinterpret the gesture. When a dog growls, it is saying, "Keep away!" When a cat purrs, it is saying, "Come and pet me; let's have a game." To a cat, the dog's growling may sound like a purr; the cat will go up to the dog. Then there will be a fight. It is hardly surprising that dogs and cats do not trust each other.

Defense and attack

A creature that wants to show its enemy how fierce and strong it is will make itself look as big as possible. The cat fluffs up its fur. This makes it look much bigger. The raised tail looks like a fat brush when its fur is bristling—a brush that could hit quite hard. The back is arched, and the cat stands sideways so that its enemy sees as much of it as possible. You can tell when a cat is getting ready to defend itself. Its teeth are bared, its pupils widened, its ears laid back, its fur on end, and it is in a crouching position.

The next step, when defense is about to become attack, is for the cat to hold its head at a slanting angle, narrow its pupils, erect its ears and point them forward, arch its back, and hold its tail stiffly downwards. At this point a dog facing it will generally run away. A cat will often attack just to make its opponent back off long enough for the cat to escape. But if kittens are threatened a mother cat will attack almost anything to protect them, and will often drive off quite large animals.

The Cat and its Language

Body language

Ritual stretching (cat feels unobserved and at ease)

Cat feels threatened: first signs of defensive posture (tail raised, fur bristling)

Ritual washing (cat feels unobserved and at ease)

Cat in defensive posture

Cat on heat, ready to mate

Cat in happy and confiding mood

Man and the cat

When a cat wants something from a human it knows, it makes the sounds we call mewing and generally write as "meow." Cats mew only at human beings. They do not use the sound for communicating with each other. There are different kinds of mewing. A cat may utter short, single sounds, or demanding yowls. In fact, there is a whole vocabulary of meows. Constant mewing is a demand for the cat to be fed or let out.

Purring tells humans that a cat is feeling contented. We do not know a great deal about the purr. But since small kittens first purr when they are suckling their mother's milk, we think that purring is their language of love. In time, cats stop purring at each other and purr only when they are with humans. When a cat rubs gently against your legs, it is asking you to notice it. It will also raise its tail straight up in the air as a sign of greeting. Licking a human hand is another sign of a cat's affection. So is the rubbing of a cat's head against a human's legs, arms, or face (usually forehead to forehead or nose to nose). This particular gesture is not kept for humans. Male and female cats rub heads to show that they like each other.

If a cat hisses it is annoyed. If the hissing turns to a low growl, it means that the cat is not afraid and is about to attack. The attack itself is accompanied by a high-pitched yowl.

The cat loves sitting on a human lap. Once on someone's lap, a cat feels safe, and it will generally jump straight up without asking if it is welcome. When a cat sitting on your lap kneads you with a constant and gentle movement of its paws, it is going back to its own kittenhood. The same kneading movement is used by the kittens when they are suckling to help themselves get more milk from their mother. The cat does not forget this gesture in later life. It can be taken as a sign of friendship.

The Cat and its Language

The language of the cat's head, eyes and whiskers

Calm, poised

Tense, concentrating

Alarmed and threatening

Threatening and just about to attack

The Whiskers: normal position

in motion

when cat is alarmed or in danger

Interesting Facts about Cats

Our earliest information about cats

The earliest information we have about cats dates from around 6000 B.C. Small statues of women with cats dating from this time have been found in Turkey. But we think it was in Egypt that cats became household pets for the first time, about 2000 B.C., during the rule of the Pharaohs when the Pyramids were built. The Egyptians called the cat Miu, and later Mau.

The strange battle of the cats

When the Persian King Cambyses was trying to capture the Egyptian city of Pelusion, he thought of a trick. He made his men tie cats to their shields. The Egyptians, who would not kill the sacred animals, dared not attack Cambyses and his army.

Sacred cats

About a thousand years later, around 950 B.C., the cat was worshiped in Egypt as a divine animal. It is, after all, a small relation of the lion, and was declared sacred to please the lion goddess Bast. Bast had a whole city of her own built for her, called Bubastis.

Ancient graves of cats

Graves containing many thousands of cat mummies (the embalmed bodies of cats) have been found near the holy city of Bubastis. Cats were sacred to the ancient Egyptians even after they were dead.

The Prophet's pet

The prophet Mohammed, founder of the religion of Islam, was devoted to his cat Muessa. One day she was asleep in the wide sleeve of his robe when Mohammed was called to prayer. Rather than disturb Muessa he cut off his sleeve so that she could go on sleeping. Today, many Mohammedans believe that people who dislike cats were rats themselves in an earlier existence.

Black cats

Witches, as shown in pictures and described in fairy tales, are supposed to have black cats perched on their backs or riding on their broomsticks. Of course it is ridiculous to think black cats are creatures of the Devil, or to suppose that there were ever real witches working real magic. But there were many such superstitions in the Middle Ages. Thousands of innocent women were burned as witches in medieval times, and their cats died with them. Even today some people think it is unlucky for a

black cat to cross your path—but others are equally sure that black cats bring luck!

Cats in our language and literature

Some people are very fond of cats, while others dislike them a great deal. No doubt it was one of the latter sort who first called a sly, spiteful person "catty." We say it is "raining cats and dogs" when it is raining very hard, and that something very funny is "enough to make a cat laugh," perhaps because cats are naturally very dignified animals. However, everyone knows about the grinning Cheshire Cat in Lewis Carroll's *Alice in Wonderland.* Another well-known cat in literature is the heroine of Edward Lear's *The Owl and the Pussycat,* while T.S. Eliot wrote a whole book of comic poems called *Old Possum's Book of Practical Cats.*

Cats: world records

The heaviest cat in the world is said to have weighed 41.8 pounds (19 kilos). A cat's normal weight is 11 pounds (5 kilos). The oldest cat lived to be 36 (a cat normally lives to be 15 to 20 years old). The biggest litter of kittens ever recorded was 13 (normal number: 2 to 6 kittens). The record for having kittens is held by a cat who was said to have had more than

400 over 17 years. We do not know how long cats can live without food, but a cat shut in a ventilation shaft in London survived there for a month and a half. In America a cat was shut up by accident inside a crate taking parts of a machine to Egypt by sea. When the crate was opened in Cairo 41 days later, out jumped the cat, along with four black kittens born during the crossing. The mother cat had kept herself and her kittens alive by licking the grease smeared on the machine parts to protect them. There are many tales of

cats covering long distances to return to their former owners or their old homes. Scientists have discovered that such stories may be true. A cat on its travels takes its bearings from the light and color around it, and the sounds it can pick up over many miles, as if by a kind of radar. One cat is said to have followed its owner from Boston to Chicago, a distance of more than 930 miles (about 1,500 kilometers), which would surely be a world record for a cat!

Tailless cats

Many tailless cats are supposed to have originated on the Isle of Man in the Irish Sea. But since tailless cats are found in many different parts of the world, it is not certain whether this belief is true. Many tailless cats hop like rabbits instead of running in an ordinary cat-like way, because they have no tails to balance them.

Pedigree cats

Pedigree cats for showing have been bred only for the last hundred years or so. Over that period breeders have succeeded in raising more than fifty new varieties from what were originally three long-haired and nine short-haired breeds of cats. If pedigree cats of two different breeds mate, the resulting kittens will not be a new breed, but are just ordinary household cats.

Index